The X Games:
Skateboarding's Greatest Event

by Jeff Savage

Capstone *press*

Mankato, Minnesota

Edge Books are published by Capstone Press
151 Good Counsel Drive, P.O. Box 669, Mankato, Minnesota 56002
www.capstonepress.com

Library of Congress Cataloging-in-Publication Data
Savage, Jeff, 1961–
    The X Games: skateboarding's greatest event / by Jeff Savage.
        p. cm.—(Edge books. Skateboarding)
    Includes bibliographic references and index.
    ISBN-13: 978-0-7368-2707-2 (hardcover)
    ISBN-10: 0-7368-2707-2 (hardcover)
    ISBN-13: 978-0-7368-6182-3 (softcover pbk.)
    ISBN-10: 0-7368-6182-3 (softcover pbk.)
    1. Skateboarding—Juvenile literature. 2. ESPN X-Games—Juvenile
literature. I. Title. II. Series.
GV859.8.S28 2005
796.22—dc22   2004000666

Summary: Discusses the history of skateboarding at the ESPN X Games
    including former and new stars of the sport.

Editorial Credits
James Anderson, editor; Timothy Halldin, series designer; Enoch Peterson, book
    designer; Jo Miller, photo researcher; Eric Kudalis, product planning editor

Photo Credits
AP/Wide World Photos/Dan Loh, 21
Corbis/NewSport/Steve Boyle, 27; NewSport/X Games IX/Matt A Brown, 6–7,
    19, 28
Getty Images/Allsport/Ezra Shaw, 24; David Leeds, 4; Ezra Shaw, 16; Hulton
    Archive, 10; Stanley Chou, 15, 20; Tom Hauck, cover
Isaac Hernandez, 8, 22
Patrick Batchelder, 12

**Edge Books thanks Tod Swank, member, Board of Directors, International
Association of Skateboard Companies, for his assistance in preparing this book.**

1 2 3 4 5 6 09 08 07 06 05 04

Table of Contents

Hawk (right) and Macdonald were stars of vert doubles.

CHAPTER ONE

What Are the X Games?

Tony Hawk has been called the king of the X Games. He has won 16 medals in the X Games. He has won more than any other skater. In 1995, he won the first X Games vert event and placed second in the street event. Hawk has won medals in vert skating, street skating, vert best trick, and vert doubles.

Hawk and Andy Macdonald are one of the best doubles vert skating pairs in X Games history. They won X Games gold medals in vert doubles every year from 1997 to 2002.

Learn About

- **The X Games king**
- **Importance of the games**
- **Sponsors**

Hawk landed a 900 at the 1999 Summer X Games. He spun two and one-half times in midair. He was the first skater to do the trick at a major event. But the trick didn't count. He landed the trick after his time had expired.

Tony Hawk may have taken his last X Games run in 2003.

Hawk landed the 900 again in 2003. This time the trick was within his contest time. After the run, Hawk said that he would no longer take part in X Games vert competitions.

About the X Games

The best action sports athletes in the world compete at the X Games. They try to win medals and prize money. The X Games is held over several days twice each year. Hundreds of thousands of fans attend the X Games and millions more watch the action on TV.

Skateboarding is one of the most popular sports in the X Games. Skaters compete in street, park, and vert skating events.

Skaters practice all year to get to the X Games. They know that sponsors watch the X Games. Sponsors are companies that pay skaters to advertise their products. Sponsors pay for skaters' clothes, gear, and equipment.

Hawk (right) and Macdonald won gold in vert doubles.

Early skaters practiced in pools at skateparks.

CHAPTER TWO

X Games History

People skated long before the X Games. Skaters in southern California skated in empty backyard swimming pools in the 1960s. In the 1970s, skateparks were built to take the place of pools. Skateboarding became popular. Skaters formed groups. These groups grew. Soon skateboarding organizations held contests at skateparks around the country.

Learn About

- ⬭ **Early skating**
- ⬭ **ESPN**
- ⬭ **The Extreme Games**

The Birth of the X Games

The X Games started in 1995. ESPN TV programmer Ron Semiao came up with the idea. Semiao knew that kids liked skateboarding, BMX, motocross, and in-line skating. Semiao thought ESPN should host a huge contest for all of these extreme sports.

The first X Games was called the Extreme Games. It was held in Newport and Providence, Rhode Island. The event lasted 10 days. At least 198,000 people came to see the contests.

Changes in the X Games

The Extreme Games was popular. ESPN officials then made some changes. After the first year, they changed the name of the contest to the X Games. They wanted a name that could be recognized around the world. After the second year, the site of the X Games was changed. The location has switched every two years since. The X Games has been held in San Diego, San Francisco, Philadelphia, and Los Angeles.

The first X Games was called the Extreme Games.

Some events at the 2003 Summer X Games were shown on live TV for the first time on the ABC network. X Games officials also charged admission that year. Fans paid $5 for a ticket. Almost 40,000 people came to the X Games each day.

More X Games

The X Games has become so popular that other events have been created. Two years after the original X Games, ESPN created the Winter X Games. The Winter X Games has sports like snowboarding, skiing, and snowmobiling.

ESPN also holds X Games events in other parts of the world. The first Asian X Games was held in 1998 in Phuket, Thailand. In 2002, the first Latin American X Games was held in Rio de Janeiro, Brazil. In 2003, a team competition called the X Games Global Championship was created.

More than 200 athletes take part in the Asian X Games each year.

Vert skating is a popular X Games event.

CHAPTER THREE

X Games Events

Skateboarding events at the X Games have changed since the first contest in 1995. Some events no longer take place. New events have been added. The two most popular events are the two main styles of skating, vert and street.

X Games Events

Vert skating takes place on a vert ramp, or halfpipe. The ramp is U-shaped. Skaters call it a halfpipe because its shape is like half of a pipe. The name vert comes from the word vertical, which means up and down.

Learn About

- Skating styles
- Scoring
- Women's vert

Street skating takes place on a street course. These courses have obstacles that can be found on city streets and sidewalks. The courses have benches, railings, stairs, and ramps.

Park skating is similar to street skating. Park courses also have other obstacles, such as miniramps and bowls.

In vert and street events, skaters take turns doing moves. Each turn is called a run. Judges score each skater's run. The skater with the highest score wins each event. Judges give scores based on creativity, difficulty, and style. At the 2003 X Games, each athlete had three 45-second runs in the vert contest. Street skaters had three 75-second runs.

Park skaters show off their moves on the park course.

Other Events

Throughout X Games history, organizers have added events other than street and vert. X Games officials decide which events will take place each year. In the 1995 Extreme Games, the four skateboard events were vert, street, street best trick, and high air. In 1997, vert doubles was added. Two skaters performed at the same time as a team. They sometimes traded boards in midair.

Many fans watch street skating events.

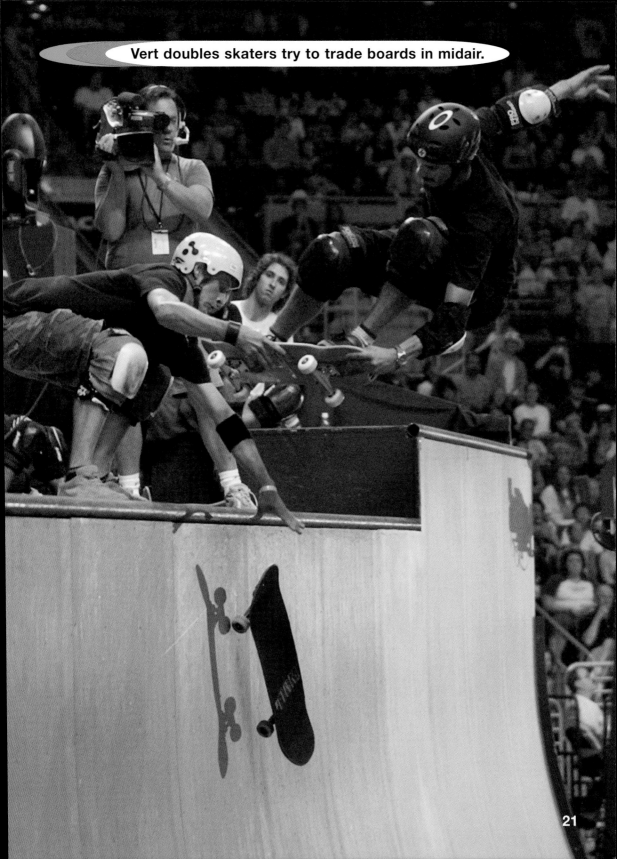

Vert doubles skaters try to trade boards in midair.

Cara-Beth Burnside is a popular female vert skater.

In 1999, vert best trick was added. During this event, Tony Hawk performed a 900 for the first time in the X Games.

In 2000, X Games officials added the park event. Park skating is similar to the street contest. The park event is held in a skatepark. The skatepark has miniramps, railings, and bowls.

Women's vert was added in 2003. The world's best female skaters took part in the contest. Cara-Beth Burnside won the gold medal, and Jen O'Brien won the silver medal. Lyn-Z Adams Hawkins won the bronze.

More female skaters are taking to the vert ramp each year. X Games officials predict that women's vert skating will be a major event in the future.

Macdonald (top) and Hawk last won doubles in 2003.

CHAPTER FOUR

X Games Champions

In the first eight years of the X Games, 40 gold medals were awarded to the top skaters. Eight skaters have been champions more than once. Among Tony Hawk's medals, 10 have been gold. Andy Macdonald has won eight gold medals.

Major Medal Winners

Hawk and Macdonald teamed up to win vert doubles six years in a row. The event was not held in 1996, the only year Hawk did not win a gold medal.

Learn About

- Tony Hawk
- Eric Koston
- Ryan Sheckler

He finished second in vert that year. The gold medal winner was Macdonald. The two skaters are good friends who live near each other. Sometimes they practice together on a halfpipe in Hawk's backyard.

Hawk and Macdonald stopped competing in vert doubles in 2003. That year, Bucky Lasek and Bob Burnquist won. Lasek and Burnquist also live near each other and practice together.

Eric Koston became a multiple gold medal winner when he won the 2003 street event. Koston competed in front of his hometown crowd in Los Angeles.

Rodil de Aruajo Jr. has won the most street gold medals. He has won six gold medals in his career. In 2002, he won three gold medals.

Trivia

Huge skateparks and vert ramps are built for X Games events. The vert ramp used at the 2003 X Games in Los Angeles was 118 feet (36 meters) long. It is the largest ramp in contest history.

Bob Burnquist skated to win silver at the 2002 X Games.

Rising Stars

Two younger skaters are Shaun White and Ryan Sheckler. White was 16 years old when he took sixth place in the 2003 vert event. Many fans call Sheckler the next Tony Hawk. Sheckler was 13 years old when he competed in his first X Games. Sheckler won the gold medal in the 2003 skateboard park event. He beat 19 other skaters.

Sheckler's win at the 2003 X Games caused many fans to notice young skaters. As skating grows more popular, some of the well-known stars are stepping aside to share the X Games spotlight. Some, like Tony Hawk, may work at the X Games as announcers. Millions of people will watch future X Games as Hawk and others introduce skateboarding's next superstars.

Ryan Sheckler is the youngest skater to win an X Games gold medal.

Glossary

admission (ad-MISH-shuhn)—a fee charged to see an event

compete (kuhm-PEET)—to try to do better than others in a contest

competition (kom-pu-TISH-uhn)—a contest

creativity (kree-ay-TIV-it-ee)—being able to make new things

difficulty (DIF-uh-kuhlt-ee)—how hard or easy something is

programmer (PROH-gram-uhr)—a person who decides which shows will be on TV

sponsor (SPON-sur)—a company that pays a skater to advertise a product

Read More

Blomquist, Christopher. *Skateboarding in the X Games.* Kid's Guide to the X Games. New York: PowerKids Press, 2003.

Doeden, Matt. *Skateparks: Grab Your Skateboard.* Skateboarding. Mankato, Minn.: Capstone Press, 2002.

Savage, Jeff. *Tony Hawk: Skateboarding Legend.* Skateboarding. Mankato, Minn.: Edge Books, 2005.

Internet Sites

FactHound offers a safe, fun way to find Internet sites related to this book. All of the sites on FactHound have been researched by our staff.

Here's how:

1. Visit *www.facthound.com*
2. Type in this special code **0736827072** for age-appropriate sites. Or enter a search word related to this book for a more general search.
3. Click on the **Fetch It** button.

FactHound will fetch the best sites for you!

Index